The ME in ChaMEleon

By Jenny Jinks

Illustrated by Gal Weizman

Cam loved being a chameleon.

He could make himself look however he wanted.

He could make all kinds of colours and shapes and patterns all over his body.

One day he would be bright purple, then the next he would be blue and stripy. Cam was always making himself stand out.

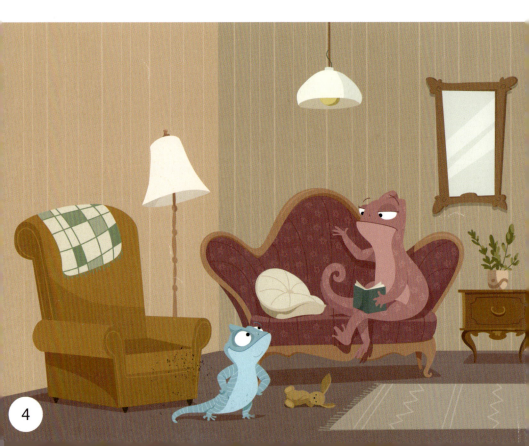

The **ME** in
ChaMEleon

'The ME in ChaMEleon'
An original concept by Jenny Jinks
© Jenny Jinks

Illustrated by Gal Weizman

Published by MAVERICK ARTS PUBLISHING LTD
Studio 11, City Business Centre, 6 Brighton Road,
Horsham, West Sussex, RH13 5BB
© Maverick Arts Publishing Limited February 2021
+44 (0)1403 256941

A CIP catalogue record for this book is available at the British Library.

ISBN 978-1-84886-763-5

www.maverickbooks.co.uk

This book is rated as: Purple Band (Guided Reading)

"That's not what you are supposed to do," said Cam's mum.

"You should use your colours to blend in, like everyone else," said Cam's dad.

"But I don't want to be like everyone else," said Cam. "I want to be me."

He liked to be bright and bold and different.

Cam was always doing things his own way. Even at school. His favourite subject was art. He loved making all his favourite colours and patterns. All of Cam's friends did their painting on big bits of paper. But not Cam...

Cam didn't need paper to do his art. Everyone laughed at him, but he didn't mind. He liked doing things his way.

"That's not what you are supposed to do," said the teacher. But she didn't really mind. They all loved Cam's bright patterns.

One day, the class were going on a field trip

into the jungle.

It was a long walk through the forest,

and there were lots of dangers on the way.

"Remember," said the teacher. "Keep together, stay quiet. And if you spot any trouble you must hide."

Everyone walked quietly through the bushes.

But not Cam...

Cam walked along, tapping his feet and humming a song. His colourful skin was flashing brightly.

"Shhh! That's not what you are supposed to do," said the teacher.

But soon they were all marching in time,

humming along to Cam's song. It made

the long walk much more fun.

The class had a great day out in the jungle.

They learnt all about the plants and the

animals. And they even had time for a game

of hide and seek.

Cam hid in the trees, but his bright colours

stood out for everyone to see.

"Found you!" Eldon said straight away.

Everyone laughed.

"That's not what you are supposed to do," said Mona. "Cam, you should blend in! You'll never win like that."

Cam just shrugged. He didn't care about winning. He knew he could blend in and hide if he wanted to. But he didn't want to. He wanted to be bright and colourful.

The sun was going down and it was time to go home. They all marched back through the bushes, humming along to Cam's song.

Suddenly, the teacher heard rustling in the bushes.

"Danger!" said the teacher. "Everybody
keep quiet and find somewhere to hide.
You know what to do."

Eldon tried to hide. But he wasn't very good at it.

Mona rushed up a tree to hide. But she wasn't very good at being quiet.

The whole class tried their best to hide.

"What about Cam?" Eldon whispered.

But nobody could find him.

This time, Cam did exactly what he was supposed to do. He used his special skill to blend in with the bushes. Nobody could see him at all.

A tiger prowled through the trees. He could hear a noise. He could smell his dinner. He saw something shaking in the bushes, and something rustling in the trees.

There were animals all around him, trying to hide. The perfect feast for a hungry tiger.

Cam stayed still and didn't make a sound.

Just like he was supposed to.

He watched the tiger walk right past him,

and he knew he was safe.

Cam sighed with relief.

But the danger wasn't over yet...

While Cam could hide easily in the jungle, his friends could not. He could see them easily. And so could the tiger.

The tiger prowled closer and closer to Cam's friends.

Cam knew what he was supposed to do. He should stay quiet and hidden, just like they had been taught. But his friends were in danger. He couldn't just leave them. So, just as the tiger was about pounce...

"Waaaaaah!" shouted Cam. He tapped his feet, hummed his tune, and made his skin as bright and colourful as he possibly could.

The tiger was shocked. He stopped still.

He had no idea what was happening.

Cam couldn't believe it. His plan was working!

Cam tapped and hummed louder and louder.

His colours got brighter and his patterns

flashed faster.

The tiger was terrified. And he wasn't hungry

anymore. He ran far away.

Slowly, everyone came out of their hiding places. Cam's teacher did not look happy.

"Cam, that was not what you are supposed to do," she said.

Cam hung his head. He was sure he was about to be in big trouble.

"But you have shown us that there is

more than one way to do things.

Your creativity saved us today."

"You're a hero, Cam," everyone said.

"I'm not a hero," Cam smiled. "I'm just me."

Quiz

1. What is Cam's favourite subject at school?
a) Art
b) Maths
c) Science

2. Where does the class go for their field trip?
a) The desert
b) The mountains
c) The jungle

3. What game did they play while on the field trip?
a) Tag
b) Hide and seek
c) Football

4. What is the danger that everyone hides from?

a) A tiger

b) A lion

c) A spider

5. What did Cam do to the tiger?

a) He talked to it

b) He helped it

c) He terrified it

Turn over for answers

Book Bands for Guided Reading

The Institute of Education book banding system is a scale of colours that reflects the various levels of reading difficulty. The bands are assigned by taking into account the content, the language style, the layout and phonics. Word, phrase and sentence level work is also taken into consideration.

Maverick Early Readers are a bright, attractive range of books covering the pink to white bands. All of these books have been book banded for guided reading to the industry standard and edited by a leading educational consultant.

To view the whole Maverick Readers scheme, visit our website at www.maverickearlyreaders.com

Or scan the QR code above to view our scheme instantly!

Quiz Answers: 1a, 2c, 3b, 4a, 5c